To:

From

D0368868

Sisters

Written and compiled by Claudine Gandolfi

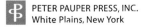

PETER PAUPER PRESS, INC.
White Plains, New York

To Michele,
my sister, my shadow, my friend

Photo credits appear on page 81

Designed by La Shae V. Ortiz

Copyright © 2008
Peter Pauper Press, Inc.
202 Mamaroneck Avenue
White Plains, NY 10601
All rights reserved
ISBN 978-1-59359-894-5
Printed in China
7 6 5 4 3 2 1
Visit us at www.peterpauper.com

Sisters

INTRODUCTION

What can be said of the bond that
sisters share? It can be a closeness
beyond compare or, at times, a little
too close for comfort. Our shared
rooms, "borrowed" clothes, mutual
secrets, disagreements, and fights
become threads of memory that
weave our lives together. As sisters,
we know that no matter what happens
between us, we will always have
each other.

C. G.

The best thing
about having a sister
was that I always
had a friend.

CALI RAE TURNER

*A sister is
a little bit of
childhood that
can never
be lost.*

MARION C. GARRETTY

Your siblings are the only people in the world who know what it's like to have been brought up the way you were.

BETSY COHEN

Having a sister is like having a best friend you can't get rid of. You know whatever you do, they'll still be there.

AMY LI

There is something so physical about sisterhood; some body-memory, too deep for words.

KENNEDY FRASER

No one can understand you like your sister. She's comprised of all the same parts you are.

My sister and I
never engaged in
sibling rivalry.
Our parents weren't
that crazy about
either one of us.

ERMA BOMBECK

*A sister is a gift
to the heart,
a friend to the
spirit, a golden
thread to the
meaning of life.*

ISADORA JAMES

To have a loving relationship with a sister is not simply to have a buddy or confidante—it is to have a soul mate for life.

VICTORIA SECUNDA

My sisters and I have
dinner-table debates about
whether it's better to establish a
career first or plan a family first.
But the discussions are really just
for fun, since we're all so
different we couldn't have
imitated each other
if we'd tried.

KATHY SPARKMAN

My sister accommodates me, never reproaches me with her doctrine, never tries to change me. She accepts and loves me, despite our differences.

JOY HARJO

Whatever you do they will love you; even if they don't love you they are connected to you until you die. You can be boring and tedious with sisters, whereas you have to put on a good face with friends.

DEBORAH MOGGACH

There is a space within sisterhood for likeness and difference, for the subtle differences that challenge and delight; there is space for disappointment— and surprise.

CHRISTINE DOWNING

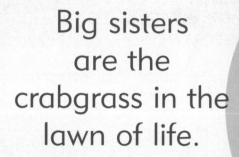

Big sisters
are the
crabgrass in the
lawn of life.

CHARLES M. SCHULZ

To most people,
my sister and I didn't
seem to have much in
common; but I knew ...
that we were
remarkably alike.

KATHLEEN NORRIS

If sisters were free
to express how they
really feel, parents would
hear this:
*"Give me all the attention
and all the toys and send
Rebecca to live with
Grandma."*

LINDA SUNSHINE

When mom and dad
don't understand,
a sister always will.

AUTHOR UNKNOWN

I suppose there are sisters who don't compete. I have never met one.

LISA GRUNWALD

How do people
make it through life
without a sister?

SARA COPENING

"My dear Jane!"
exclaimed Elizabeth, "you are too
good. Your sweetness and
disinterestedness are really
angelic; I do not know what
to say to you. I feel as if I had
never done you justice,
or loved you as you deserve."

JANE AUSTEN,
Pride and Prejudice

Is solace anywhere
more comforting than
in the arms of a sister?

ALICE WALKER

For there is no friend like a sister

In calm or stormy weather;

To cheer one on the tedious way,

To fetch one if one goes astray,

To lift one if one totters down,

To strengthen whilst one stands.

CHRISTINA ROSSETTI,
Goblin Market

It is true that I was born in Iowa, but I can't speak for my twin sister.

ABIGAIL VAN BUREN

One of the best things about being an adult is the realization that you can share with your sister and still have plenty for yourself.

BETSY COHEN

You can kid the world. But not your sister.

CHARLOTTE GRAY

A sister shares childhood memories and grown-up dreams.

AUTHOR UNKNOWN

I cannot deny that, now I am without your company I feel not only that I am deprived of a very dear sister, but that I have lost half of myself.

BEATRICE D'ESTE,
from a letter to her sister Isabella

As young children,
my sisters and I were close.
I enjoyed being the oldest,
showing them around,
protecting them. When
a bully who sat across from
Susan at the schoolroom
table kicked her legs
black-and-blue, I beat him
up in the playground.

PATRICIA IRELAND

Sisters touch your heart in ways no other could. Sisters share their hopes, fears, love, everything they have.

CARRIE BAGWELL

Ashley is the part of my mom that my mom likes best. She's intellectual, organized, such a hostess.

WYNONNA JUDD

If you and your sister
take time to do things
one-on-one, away from
the extended family,
a new pattern of dealing
with each other—and a
new friendship—is free
to emerge.

KIM WRIGHT WILEY

Sisters—they share the agony
and the exhilaration.
As youngsters they may
share popsicles, chewing gum,
hair dryers, and bedrooms.
When they grow up, they share
confidences, careers,
and children, and some even
chat for hours every day.

ROXANNE BROWN

For when three sisters
love each other with such
sincere affection, the one does
not experience sorrow, pain,
or affliction of any kind,
but the others' heart wishes
to relieve, and vibrates in
tenderness. Like a well-organized
musical instrument.

ELIZABETH SHAW,
sister of Abigail Adams and Mary Cranch

My oldest sister,
Alice Lynn Foran . . . is the
rock, the one you can call
at three in the morning,
and she'll always be ready
to help in any way.

REBA MCENTIRE

Sisters function
as safety nets
in a chaotic
world simply by
being there for
each other.

CAROL SALINE

A sister can be
your conscience,
your confidante,
and your champion.

We acquire friends and we make enemies, but our sisters come with the territory.

EVELYN LOEB

We had problems for a long time because we both thought we were Mom's favorite child. We talked over our feelings about this four years ago and realized it didn't matter who was the favorite. Now we're just happy we have each other.

ANONYMOUS,
*quoted by Francine Klagsbrun in
Mixed Feelings*

Mom sent me to the pantry for flour and I put a half-eaten Milky Way bar on the counter. When I came back, Sheila was eating it. Sheila is the one person on earth who can easily reduce me to the emotions and mentality of a six-year-old.

DEBORAH PERRY

*I asked for her advice
and help. It was a
homecoming of sorts.
I can still recall the
fullness in her voice when
she told me how very, very
touched she was that at last
I was letting her in.*

MARCIA ANN GILLESPIE,
about her sister Charlene

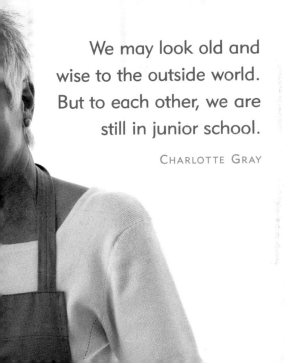

We may look old and
wise to the outside world.
But to each other, we are
still in junior school.

CHARLOTTE GRAY

Only a sister
can compare the sleek body
that now exists with the chubby
body hidden underneath.
Only a sister knows
about former pimples, failing
math, and underwear
kicked under the bed.

LAURA TRACY

If your sister is in
a tearing hurry
to go out and cannot
catch your eye,
she's wearing
your best sweater.

PAM BROWN

Even when my sister
and I are separated by
continents, we are
moving through time
in parallel tracks.

KENNEDY FRASER

A ministering
angel shall my
sister be.

WILLIAM SHAKESPEARE,
Hamlet

I wish dolphin were
by my side, in a bath, bright
blue, with her tail curled.
But then I've always been
in love with her since I
was a green eyed brat
under the nursery table,
and so shall remain in
my extreme senility.

VIRGINIA WOOLF,
about her sister Vanessa Bell

Bessie and I have been together
since time began, or so it seems.
Bessie is my little sister,
only she's not so little.
She is 101 years old, and
I'm 103. . . . After so long,
we are in some ways
like one person.

SARAH L. "SADIE" DELANY

A sister can be
seen as someone
who is both ourselves
and very much not
ourselves—a special
kind of double.

TONI MORRISON

I wrote a long letter to Santa Claus and said that I had been particularly good that year and felt I was quite deserving. I ended with, "I look forward to seeing you." Then I added, "P.S. My turtle died two days ago. I hope my sister's turtle dies, too."

FRANCINE KLAGSBRUN,
Mixed Feelings

She never judges me,
and through the many
rehab treatments she's
always been supportive.
Not in a caretaking way,
but she's always wanted
me to be all right.

CARRIE MORROW,
about her sister, Jennifer Jason Leigh

We'd fall asleep holding onto each other's hair.

ASHLEY JUDD,
about her sister Wynonna

*Listening to my sister
sing has been one
of the greatest gifts
of my life.*

NORMAN BUCKLEY,
brother of Betty Buckley

What's the good of news if you haven't a sister to share it?

JENNY DEVRIES

One of the nicest things about those early years on the bus was being together with Louise and Irlene, just as we had been as children. . . . I was still able to play Big Sister to the hilt, coaching my sisters about their roles in the band but also relying on them for help with Matthew.

BARBARA MANDRELL

Emily's love was poured out on Anne, as Charlotte's was on her. But the affection among all the three was stronger than either death or life.

ELIZABETH. GASKELL,
on the Brontë sisters

Never praise a
sister to a sister
in the hope of your
compliments reaching
the proper ears.

RUDYARD KIPLING

If you don't understand how a woman could both love her sister dearly and want to wring her neck at the same time, then you were probably an only child.

LINDA SUNSHINE

She takes my hand
and leads me along
paths I would
not have dared
explore alone.

MAYA V. PATEL

My sisters are guaranteed friends for life. . . . There's never a reason to hurt your sisters. Never was, never will be.

KELLY TURLINGTON

You should never look down on a sister except to pick her up.

Sisters may share the same mothers and fathers but often appear to come from different families.

EVELYN BEILENSON

Chance made
us sisters, hearts
made us friends.

I'm the watcher.
I like to observe and
Joan very much likes to
participate. She likes to be
center stage, and I like to sit
in the background.

JACKIE COLLINS

*The mildest,
drowsiest
sister has been
known to turn
tiger if her sibling
is in trouble.*

CLARA ORTEGA

In the cookies of
life, sisters are
the chocolate chips.

AUTHOR UNKNOWN

Photo Credits